Fall Leaves

Katie Peters

GRL Consultants,
Diane Craig and Monica Marx,
Certified Literacy Specialists

Lerner Publications ◆ Minneapolis

Lerner Publications Company
A division of Lerner Publishing Group, Inc.
241 First Avenue North
Minneapolis, MN 55401 USA

For reading levels and more information, look up this title at www.lernerbooks.com.

Main body text set in Memphis Pro 24/39
Typeface provided by Linotype.

Photo Acknowledgments
The images in this book are used with the permission of: © Shutterstock, pp. 3, 6–7, 8–9, 10–11, 14–15, 16 (top left), 16 (bottom left), 16 (bottom right); © iStockphoto, pp. 4–5, 12–13, 16 (top right)

Front cover: © Shutterstock

Library of Congress Cataloging-in-Publication Data

Names: Peters, Katie, author.
Title: Fall leaves / Katie Peters.
Description: Minneapolis : Lerner Publications, [2020] | Series: Science all around me (Pull ahead readers - Nonfiction) | Includes index. | Audience: Age 4–7. | Audience: K to Grade 3.
Identifiers: LCCN 2018058181 (print) | LCCN 2019000018 (ebook) | ISBN 9781541562356 (eb pdf) | ISBN 9781541558724 (lb : alk. paper) | ISBN 9781541573444 (pb : alk. paper)
Subjects: LCSH: Leaves—Juvenile literature. | Fall foliage—Juvenile literature. | Autumn—Juvenile literature.
Classification: LCC QK649 (ebook) | LCC QK649 .P477 2020 (print) | DDC 581.4/8—dc23

LC record available at https://lccn.loc.gov/2018058181

Manufactured in the United States of America
1 – CG – 7/15/19

Contents

Fall Leaves

It is fall.

It gets cold in the fall.

The leaves change color.
Look at the colors.

The wind blows the leaves.

The leaves fall.

I rake the leaves.

I lie in the leaves.

I throw the leaves.

Did You See It?

leaves

lie

rake

throw

Index